JOSHUA HALLS

The SOUND Before the BREAKTHROUGH

A Prophetic Call for Worshippers to Arise and Shake the Nation

Copyright notice: © 2025 by Joshua Halls

Rights statement: "All rights reserved. No part of this publication may be reproduced, distributed, or transmitted in any form or by any means, including photocopying, recording, or other electronic or mechanical methods, without the prior written permission of the publisher, except in the case of brief quotations embodied in critical reviews and certain other noncommercial uses permitted by copyright law."

Scripture taken from the New King James Version®. Copyright © 1982 by Thomas Nelson. Used by permission. All rights reserved.

THE HOLY BIBLE, NEW INTERNATIONAL VERSION®, NIV® Copyright © 1973, 1978, 1984, 2011 by Biblica, Inc.® Used by permission. All rights reserved worldwide.

Scripture quotations taken from the Amplified® Bible (AMP), Copyright © 2015 by The Lockman Foundation. Used by permission. lockman.org

Cover Design: Joshua Halls

Print ISBN: 978-0-646-71110-2
EBook ISBN: 978-0-646-71440-0

Published and distributed by Joshua Halls & Australian Worship Network
info@australianworshipnetwork.com.au

AUSTRALIAN **WORSHIP NETWORK**

DEDICATION

To the worshipper holding this book — may you never lose sight of the unspeakable honour and privilege it is to worship King Jesus and serve his bride. May you be captivated by the unsearchable depths of His greatness, and may your worship become a living reflection of His glory. As you yield to His Spirit in worship, I pray you experience His kingdom come, on Earth as it is in Heaven.

INDEX

	Forewords	09
1.	Can My Worship Change the Nation?	13
2.	The Sound Before the Breakthrough	19
3.	The New Sound	25
4.	The Spiritual Battle	33
5.	The Power of Declaration	39
6.	The Prophetic Sound of David's Tabernacle	53
7.	Hearing Heaven	65
8.	One Sound Many Voices	79
9.	Your Voice – Your Territory	87
10.	The Call	95
11.	A Prophetic Declaration for the Nation	99

ACTIVATIONS

1. Can My Worship Change the Nation?	106
2. Hearing Heaven's Sound	108
3. Singing Over Dry Bones	110
4. The Power of Declaration	112
5. Worshippers as Priests	114
6. Tuning In to His Voice	116
7. Sermons Into Songs	118
8. Partnering with Prophetic Words	120
9. Writing the Songs for Tomorrow	122
10. The Sound of Unity	124
11. Carrying the Presence Beyond the Church	126
12. Mapping Your Territory	128
13. Your Response	130
14. Crafting a Prophetic Declaration	132

FOREWORDS

If you have picked up this book, it's because you believe like me, that worship has always been more than just music—it is a response to who God is and a catalyst for what He is doing on the earth. As worshippers, we often sense that our songs, prayers, and declarations carry weight, but do we truly believe they can shape the spiritual landscape of a nation? I think we often fall short in our belief that our humble melodies and worship could do that. But I am constantly reminded of David the shepherd boy singing to sheep in the fields before he was leading worshipers in a tabernacle to release heaven on earth. The sound of the shepherd became a priestly and royal song heard in kingly courts, songs so powerful that we still have those words today in the Psalms.

Can our worship impact a nation? This is the question my friend Joshua Halls explores in *The Sound Before the Breakthrough*. And if anyone is qualified to write this book, it is Joshua. I have had the privilege of knowing him as a worshipper who has remained faithful in the secret place for decades. He is not just someone who talks about worship; he lives it. His life is a testament to the power of consistent, surrendered worship—both in personal devotion and in leading others into God's presence. That faithfulness gives him authority to speak on this subject, and his journey will inspire you to see your own sounds of worship in a new light.

For me, as a worship leader and songwriter now spanning many seasons in my life, I have witnessed firsthand the power of sound to shift atmospheres, bring healing, and release breakthrough. I have seen it all over Australia, in Asia and Fiji. There has not been one nation I have visited where I have not seen worship crack open something in the spirit. It is in those moments that we realize that worship is not just about singing songs; it is a prophetic act that partners with heaven to release God's purposes on the earth. This book captures that reality in a profound and practical way, reminding us that before every move of God, there is a sound—a sound that we are invited to release. What an honour and privilege!

As you read, I pray you will be stirred not just to understand this truth but to step into it. Your worship, whether in a congregation or in the quiet of your own home, carries significance. Joshua's words will challenge and encourage you to lift your voice with fresh faith, knowing that heaven responds when worshippers arise.

The question is not can our worship change the nation, but will we release the sound? I believe it will be a resounding yes as a new breed of worshippers arise for such a time as this!

Roma Waterman

Worship Leader, Songwriter, and Teacher
Founder of HeartSong Prophetic Alliance
& Wisdom at the Well

Joshua has been a much-loved member of our church family for the past 26 years and throughout that time has faithfully served as part of our worship team. Through God's grace, Joshua—together with our worship team—flows in prophetic worship, seeking to move as one with the Holy Spirit. It has been a wonderful journey, as together we endeavor to explore the depths of God's heart and to release the songs and sounds of the Spirit.

Joshua carries an expression of worship that opens, invites, and welcomes the presence of the Lord and his worship style has been greatly appreciated by leaders across our region and throughout the nation.

I am proud of Joshua. He is a son who is well loved and celebrated in our house and I am delighted and honoured to seize this opportunity to say: "Well done, son."

As you read Joshua's book, I believe you will hear—with the ear of your heart—*The Sound Before the Breakthrough*.

Kim Jones

Senior Leader,
Liberty Family Church, Gosford

CHAPTER 1

Can My Worship Change the Nation?

"You have been chosen by God for a great move of the Holy Spirit...this move of God will be the greatest move of God ever known in mankind's history, and will start towards the end of the 20th century and move into the 21st century. This move of God will start a great revival in Australia and spread throughout the world."
—Smith Wigglesworth

Australia - *"You have been chosen."* These were the words spoken by Smith Wigglesworth which for generations have echoed throughout Australia's spiritual landscape. These words have been confirmed and amplified by both international voices and local prophets, each adding their thread to a tapestry of great expectation. Ever since then, the prophetic words have not stopped, coming at what seems like an increasingly rapid pace. It's exciting!

But amidst the excitement we need to consider this - that these prophetic words without participation remain only words on a page. God seeks the cooperation of His people. This fact is evident in Scripture and throughout history as we see God in close cooperation with his people doing great things. Revivals have been started, stewarded, and even diminished by the cooperation—or lack thereof—of the people. A sobering fact when for decades, a great move of God for the nation is something that many of us have been praying and believing for.

History has also shown us that revival is marked with the sound of worship, both preemptive and in response to what God is doing. This coming prophesied move of God will be no different. If we are to be a part of this great prophesied revival then our worshippers had better rise up! We had better take up our priestly role and worship like never before on behalf of our nation. The hour for hesitation has gone, and the moment for bold and powerful worship has come. Come on worshipper… it's time!

The Birthing Place

While working as a high school teacher, I often found myself drawn to the solitude of the school's music room during spare moments. Tucked away in a separate building at the back of the school, this space became my sanctuary—a place where I could spend time freely in worship and in prayer. For me it was a sacred and holy space.

In that room stood a piano that held special significance. It was the very same instrument where, 25 years earlier as a student at the same school, I had first encountered God. Back then, I was a lost and broken teenager who found refuge behind a piano room's locked door, seeking escape from the world. Hopeless and in the midst of personal turmoil, I had nowhere to turn except towards Heaven. That is when I encountered the touch of a loving Father that changed my life.

As my daily encounters with Him increased, and the Lord began working on my heart, songs and sounds of thanksgiving and worship began to pour out of me through those keys. God heard those raw expressions and met me in my brokenness, bringing healing and restoration to countless areas of my life.

Over time, and as my daily times of hidden worship continued, I would find myself increasingly interrupted by the sound of other students knocking on the door wanting to come in. They had heard the sound of worship coming from within the confines of that small room and were drawn to it. At times there were up to half a dozen of us crammed in all singing and worshipping together as we would encounter God's presence in a rich way. God did something beautiful in me during those times. It was the birthing place for what became a life long pursuit of Him through worship.

Two and a half decades later, I found myself at the same piano, but something was different. While those early worship sessions had brought great personal encounters and transformation for myself, God was stirring something bigger. The sounds being released were no longer just for personal breakthrough—He was awakening a heart for the nation.

Can My Worship Change a Nation?

So one particular day, as I prayed and worshipped, a spontaneous melody in the form of a question emerged from deep within my spirit. *"Can my worship change a nation?"* As soon as I sang this line I knew there was something on it. This wasn't just a lyric—it was a heart cry born from both hope and doubt. Hope to see God do something great, but yet a feeling of doubt that anything I could ever offer would make a difference. This question hung in the air as I repeatedly sang it over and over. *"Can my worship change a nation?"* Leaning into this spontaneous song, it wasn't long before I heard the Holy Spirit sing back to me: *"Yes, it can, and it does!"*

Who me? My worship? "Yes it does?" How?

As the revelation of this unfolded, I remembered back to that small piano room—where the sound of worship permeated the walls and became an invitation, beckoning people to come. People came not only for the sound but for the atmosphere that was created. An atmosphere rich in God's presence—a place for life-changing encounters. It was a place where people came in empty and broken and left filled, carrying the atmosphere of Heaven into the next space. That's how it starts. That's how we change a nation. One localised act of worship at a time changing the hearts and the lives of the people.

Let me encourage you with this: It has to start somewhere, and it starts where we are right now! In our homes, churches, schools, and every other place we go. It doesn't have to be loud or extravagant (although sometimes it is) but it must change the atmosphere enough to release the Kingdom of Heaven into the earth where we are.

The Fulfillment

The fulfillment of Wigglesworth's prophecy—and countless others like it—doesn't rest solely with famous worship leaders or well-known prophetic voices. It is up to worshippers like you and I. Those that will shift the atmospheres over our own regions and areas of influence with our songs of worship. This move requires the activation of every worshipper in releasing their song and flooding the Earth with the sounds of worship.

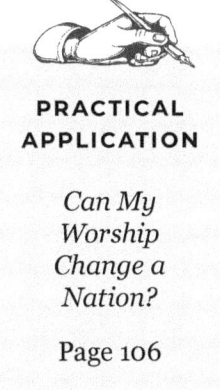

PRACTICAL APPLICATION

Can My Worship Change a Nation?

Page 106

The question today is not *"Can our worship change a nation?"* but is rather "Will we release our sound?" Will we take our places in God's army of worshippers and what role will we play in the greatest outpouring that will ever be?

As you continue to read this book, I pray that God will stir your heart to see our great nation flooded with the sound of worship!

CHAPTER 2

The Sound Before the Breakthrough

Many years ago I went to a conference seeking a time of personal refreshing—a chance to simply be a part of a congregation and be encouraged without the responsibility that came with serving. Little did I know that this was an event that would have a life-changing impact. God wanted to teach me something powerful, and ultimately every worshipper who would hear this story.

This one particular session throughout the day began conventionally enough. The worship team led us through their planned progression of songs, moving from upbeat praise to slower, more intimate worship. The standard church format we are all accustomed to. Then at a certain point in the service, when one of the more worshipful songs had come to an end, we entered what we often call a *"Selah"* moment—that brief pause where all instruments cease and God's people simply rest quietly in His presence. I can't remember the songs they sang but I remember they created such a sweet and reverent atmosphere. The people stood still in a moment of holy silence; you could have heard a pin drop. It was then that something unexpected happened.

Without warning, one of the backing singers let out a sound that caught everyone off guard—a shrill, what sounded like a Native American war cry, delivered full-voice into the microphone. If you've ever watched old Western films, you know the sound—that distinctive, throat-warbling cry that most people can't reproduce. It wasn't particularly beautiful, and in the context of a worship service, it seemed utterly bizarre.

I'll be honest: my first reaction was shock, and for a moment, I found myself becoming quite judgmental of the situation. *"Why on earth would anyone do that?"* I thought, feeling somewhat embarrassed for her. This wasn't some accident or half-hearted attempt—it was intentional and remarkably loud. My critical response, however, lasted only but a few seconds before everything changed.

What followed her "outburst" was a brief moment of silence, before—BOOM! The whole place erupted. People began to scream and jump while others danced wildly with their arms flailing. Some even ran around the auditorium while others shook and cried uncontrollably. Holy chaos had just erupted in the room! I can feel goosebumps even now as I recall the shift in the atmosphere. If you have experienced this type of move of the Spirit, you would know exactly what I am talking about. I stood there in amazement as the atmosphere transformed in a split second—the moment Heaven's atmosphere broke into the room.

All of a sudden, the drummer started to bring forth a tribal drum beat, followed shortly afterwards by the rest of the musicians. Following them came the singers with spontaneous songs and the people followed. Away we all went. From this point worship continued for another couple of hours although it only felt like twenty minutes. This was unlike anything I'd experienced before.

When this unscripted time of extended worship finally concluded and everything had seemed to settle, the guest speaker approached the microphone and asked the backing singer, *"Why did you make that sound?"* Something we had all possibly been wondering.

Her response was simple: *"I heard it, so I did it."*

Wow! That powerful statement shifted my entire perspective. This singer had heard with her spiritual ears a sound resonating in Heaven's atmosphere, and it was her radical obedience to the Holy Spirit's prompting and her willingness to reproduce that sound on Earth which shifted the atmosphere, changing the entire atmosphere of the room. It was, quite literally, the sound before the breakthrough.

Pursuing the Sound

For me, that single moment of obedience became a powerful demonstration of what can happen when one worshipper responds to Heaven's prompting without hesitation.

For me this encounter became a catalyst for a deeper journey—a quest to understand the sound that unlocks Heaven and releases it on Earth. As I began searching Scripture, I discovered a pattern: many times before something miraculous happened, before there was a shifting and a shaking, there was a sound just like I had experienced.

In Scripture we see that the walls of Jericho fell to the sound of trumpets and shouts. The songs of Paul and Silas shook prison foundations and set captives free. David's harp drove away tormenting spirits and unified worship at the dedication of Solomon's temple became a place of habitation for the manifest presence of God. These weren't isolated incidents—they were demonstrations of worship's power to shape the reality of our world and situations.

In the light of these miraculous stories I was reading I began to wonder: why aren't we witnessing these dramatic manifestations in today's church? Where are the walls coming down and the revivals in jail cells? Where is the army of worshippers shifting the destiny of our nation? I mean it's in scripture, so why aren't we seeing it?

Careful and prayerful consideration from the moment that singer released that sound up until the writing of this book has led me to a confronting conclusion... Perhaps it's us!

Perhaps, we need to examine and re-evaluate the role we play in partnering with and releasing Heaven's sound in worship. Perhaps we have diminished worship's power because we have contained it to our Sunday services and made it a mere emotional experience rather than seeking Heaven's agenda. What if we've barely scratched the surface of worship's true potential?

Just Imagine

As we explore this topic more throughout the book, I want to encourage you to raise your faith and expectation. Take a moment to consider what might happen if our worship were like the examples we see in Scripture. What could it mean for our homes, our communities, and even the nation? Imagine if a sound was released s was so powerful the entire nation fell to their knees under the weight of God's glory. I do believe it's possible, however, I also know that we need to partner with Heaven if we are to see this sound released.

PRACTICAL APPLICATION

Hearing Heaven's Sound

Page 108

CHAPTER 3

The New Sound

Throughout Scripture, we encounter a remarkable and recurring pattern: that when God's people released a sound in worship, praise and celebration, something miraculous followed. But it was not always in the same way. Like a master composer, God used specific sounds for specific moments. Our role isn't to simply replicate what worked before, but to partner with Him in releasing the new sound He desires for each season and situation.

"Behold, I am doing a new thing; now it springs forth, do you not perceive it?" —Isaiah 43:19 ESV

The question that we as worshippers need to ask ourselves is, "Are we perceiving the new and fresh sounds Heaven wants to release in our generation?"

The word "*new*" in Isaiah 43:19 is the same word used in Psalm 96:1: "*sing to the Lord a **new** song.*"

In Hebrew, the word for *new* is "chadash[1]," which means refreshed, renewed, or repaired. Singing the new song isn't just about creating unheard melodies—it's about releasing songs and sounds that carry fresh revelation, bring renewal, and restoration. The emphasis on "chadash" reveals that God isn't looking for worship for entertainment's sake, but rather for sounds that will establish His kingdom and purpose on the earth.

As worshippers, we must learn to cultivate a deeper sensitivity to these new sounds. Yesterday's expressions, while powerful in their time, may not carry the same authority for today's battles. Each season, and indeed moment, requires its own sound, its own "chadash" expression of Heaven's purposes.

Being on the cutting edge with the new sound requires great discernment and sensitivity to the Holy Spirit's leading. Sometimes the Lord calls for a shout, other times for a whisper. Sometimes for warfare, other times for waiting. Our effectiveness in worship isn't measured by volume or skill alone but by our ability to discern and release the sound Heaven is wanting to release.

The Power of the Sound

As we explore the following biblical examples, we can see that these moments of sound and song weren't random expressions

---

1. BibleHub, Strong's Hebrew: 2319

but divine partnerships—God's people discerning and releasing exactly what was needed for breakthrough in their specific circumstances. We too can learn from these biblical models. Let's have a closer look.

Sound as a Weapon: Joshua & Jericho

"When the trumpets sounded, the army shouted, and at the sound of the trumpet, when the men gave a loud shout, the wall collapsed." —Joshua 6:20 NIV

The battle of Jericho stands as perhaps the most dramatic demonstration of sound preceding supernatural breakthrough. This wasn't merely a military campaign; it was a lesson about the power of obedience and timing in releasing the prophetic sound. For six days, the Israelites marched in silence—a test of obedience and faith that would have seemed foolish to military strategists. The final breakthrough came with the continuous blowing of the trumpets and the people's unified shout seeing the walls fall flat. Strategic obedience and patience were very central to the unfolding of this powerful military victory.

At this moment, Joshua and his worshippers grasped something many modern worshippers may have forgotten: releasing the sound isn't always just about expression; sometimes it's about invasion and taking enemy territory.

Sound of Healing: David & Saul

"Whenever the spirit from God came on Saul, David would take up his lyre and play. Then relief would come to Saul; he would feel better, and the evil spirit would leave him." —1 Samuel 16:23 NIV

The account of David playing for Saul reveals another dimension entirely—worship's power to bring healing and deliverance. Once again, this isn't simply about musical talent or entertainment; it was a demonstration of how anointed sound can create an atmosphere where darkness cannot remain.

The result of David's playing was not something that happened by chance, but was something he had developed throughout the years, David had become skilled in releasing the atmosphere of Heaven through his sound. Whenever the tormenting spirit troubled Saul, David's worship brought relief. This reveals a spiritual principle: anointed worship creates an atmosphere that is hostile to darkness. The same David who fought and defeated his natural enemy Goliath with a sling understood that worship was also a weapon: a spiritual one that could drive back spiritual enemies.

The Sound before the Glory: Solomon's Temple

"The trumpeters and musicians joined in unison to give praise and thanks to the Lord. . . Then the temple of the Lord was filled

with the cloud." —2 Chronicles 5:13 NIV

The dedication of Solomon's Temple presents yet another aspect— unified worship that welcomes the manifest presence of God. Here, the emphasis falls on unity—the singers and musicians were "as one" suggesting more than mere musical synchronization but a united spiritual harmony. Their unified declaration, *"For He is good, for His mercy endures forever,"* preceded an extraordinary manifestation: the glory of God filled the temple so powerfully that the priests couldn't stand to minister. A powerful reminder that God inhabits the praises of His people (Psalm 22:3).

Sound for Prophecy: Elisha & The Minstrel

"But now bring me a musician." Then it happened, when the musician played, that the hand of the LORD came upon him." —2 Kings 3:15 NKJV

The account of Elisha calling for a musician (minstrel) reveals yet another dimension of Heaven-directed sound—its power to create space for prophetic revelation. When the musician played, the hand of the Lord came upon Elisha, and he prophesied. The anointed sound became a catalyst that enabled the prophetic to flow. Elisha knew the connection between music and the prophetic, hence his need to draw upon the gifted musicianship of the minstrel.

The Sound before Freedom: Paul & Silas

"About midnight Paul and Silas were praying and singing hymns to God, and the other prisoners were listening to them. Suddenly there was such a violent earthquake that the foundations of the prison were shaken." —Acts 16:25-26 NIV

Paul and Silas's prison worship demonstrates worship's power to bring breakthrough even in seemingly impossible moments. Despite being beaten, chained, and imprisoned, they chose to worship. The Greek word used, hymnoun, meaning *"to praise and celebrate through the singing of hymns,"* was not merely quietly humming or lamenting but worshipping in a way that opposed their current circumstances.

The results were incredible. Scripture says that while they sang, the other prisoners listened. Those listening did not actively participate in the worship, yet the chains fell off EVERYONE! The event led not only to the freedom of those imprisoned but also to the salvation of the jailer's entire family. When we grasp the fact that our worship impacts not only our own lives but those around us, how much more do we recognize the need to step out in worship.

Sound as Warfare: Jehoshaphat's Army

"After consulting the people, Jehoshaphat appointed men to sing to the Lord and to praise him for the splendor of his holiness

as they went out at the head of the army, saying: 'Give thanks to the Lord, for his love endures forever.'" —2 Chronicles 20:21

Jehoshaphat's story presents perhaps the most unconventional military strategy in history. Faced with overwhelming odds against multiple armies, he put the worship team on the front lines. This wasn't a desperate last resort; it was a deliberate strategy based on faith in God's promise: *"The battle is not yours, but God's"* (2 Chronicles 20:15 NKJV). The outcome of this victory was so great that it not only changed the destiny of the nation, but it took three days to collect the spoils.

The Pattern for Today

Considering the examples we have just read, my lingering question has been *"why do we not see and experience this kind of miraculous events today?"* I believe these accounts aren't just historical tales but are patterns for breakthrough that we in our own time should note. The challenges we face may look different from Jehoshaphat's battle or Paul & Silas's prison walls, but they can often feel just as overwhelming. The biblical pattern remains clear and consistent: the sounds of praise, worship, singing, and celebration precede the breakthrough.

CHAPTER 4

The Spiritual Battle

"For we do not wrestle against flesh and blood, but against principalities, against powers, against the rulers of the darkness of this age, against spiritual hosts of wickedness in the heavenly places." —Ephesians 6:12 NKJV

There is a real battle going on and it's a spiritual one. All you have to do is look around and see the nature of the fall and its influence coming against us from every angle. From media to politics to our education system, we see the infiltration of ideologies, schemes, and agendas that are in complete opposition to God's kingdom and His plans for mankind—something that, if we remain passive or apathetic about, will eventually overcome us.

This is why it is necessary for the church to arise and start to influence every area of society. Indeed, I would hate to think what the world would look like if it were void of the kingdom influence brought by anointed men and women of God into their sphere of influence. Those that arise and fight must do so not with natural weapons but with spiritual ones.

"For the weapons of our warfare are not carnal but mighty in God for pulling down strongholds." —2 Corinthians 10:4 NKJV

The words *"pulling"* and *"strongholds"* in the Greek are the words *"kathairesis[1]"* and *"ochyrōmaton[2]."* The word *"kathairesis"* means to take down, demolish, or destroy while the word *"ochyrōmaton"* means a fortress, strong defence, or stronghold. These spiritual weapons are able to take down, demolish, and destroy fortresses, strong defenses, and strongholds. In the Greco-Roman world, the concept of *"kathairesis"* would have been understood in both literal and metaphorical senses: the physical destruction of fortified cities during times of war as well as a metaphorical spiritual warfare context often found in the teaching of the apostles.

These spiritual weapons are powerful tools in our arsenal, and worship is one of the most potent. It is one which, as we have seen, is capable of yielding great impact and devastation to the enemy. When used with the authority we are given in Christ, we will see the Kingdom of Heaven released on the Earth in powerful ways and see the kingdom of darkness destroyed.

Jesus Has All Authority

"And Jesus came and spoke to them, saying, 'All authority has been given to Me in heaven and on earth. Go therefore and

---

1. BibleHub, Strong's Greek: 2506
2. BibleHub, Strong's Greek: 3794

make disciples of all the nations...'" —Matthew 28:18-19 NKJV

All authority in both Heaven and Earth... That encompasses everything! There is nothing that exists that is outside the authority and influence of Christ.

While Jesus has the authority, we however are the ones with the responsibility to act on His behalf and *"go and make disciples of the nations."* The Great Commission is an active outworking that every believer must play a role in. For our nation to be impacted, however, It will take worshippers who know their assignment and who will stand boldly in their authority in Christ.

Ruling and Reigning with Christ

"And God raised us up with Christ and seated us with him in the heavenly realms in Christ Jesus." —Ephesians 2:6 (NIV)

When we fight this battle, we do so knowing that, according to Scripture, our battle position is *in him*—the one who has *all* authority and power—Jesus.

This isn't something that we aspire to achieve but is a very present reality. We are already *"raised up"* and already seated *"far above all principality, and power, and might, and dominion, and every name that is named, not only in this world, but also in that which is to come"* (Ephesians 1:21). The understanding of this position is something we need to receive and accept by faith if we are to step into it with confidence.

The Keys to Heaven and Earth

"I will give you the keys of the kingdom of heaven; whatever you bind on earth will be bound in heaven, and whatever you loose on earth will be loosed in heaven." Matthew 16:19 NIV

Notice the keys are *heavenly* keys, not earthly ones. That is because the battle is won in the Spirit first. These keys have given us access to His place of power positioned right beside Christ, where we can hear His directives and the words He speaks and then go forth and speak them on His behalf as ambassadors. The words Christ speaks are powerful, even when spoken on His behalf by the saints.

From our position in Christ we need to be making some bold and powerful decrees and declarations which determine outcomes in both the spiritual and natural world.

Angel Armies

This spiritual battle is not something we have to do alone. Not only do we have the Godhead on our side, but we also have the full weight of Heaven's military forces—Heaven's angel armies.

"Bless the Lord, you His angels, Who excel in strength, who do His word, Heeding the voice of His word. Bless the Lord, all you His hosts, You ministers of His, who do His pleasure." —Psalm 103:20-21 NKJV

These armies, who excel in strength, stand ready for deployment—prepared to heed the word of the Lord. The Hebrew word for *"Heed"* is *"shama[3],"* meaning *"to hear"* or *"to listen."* It extends beyond the mere act of hearing to include understanding, paying attention, and responding appropriately, often implying obedience. The angelic armies are positioned to hear and obey the directives of Heaven without hesitation.

This should give us great boldness, for when we hear and then speak forth the word of the Lord, we can confidently know that God's angelic army stands ready to bring those directives to pass.

Knowing Your Authority

As worshippers, when we understand the spiritual dynamics of the battle we face, we are better positioned to fight with maximum efficiency. Also, understanding and taking up our position of ultimate authority in Christ is essential if we are to invade the

---

[3] BibleHub, Strong's Hebrew: 8085

enemy territory and see the nation impacted in the way we so desire. We simply cannot operate in an authority we are not aware of.

As modern day worshippers, be encouraged that you stand with the full backing of Heaven, in the full delegated authority of Christ. The spiritual position in which you stand is powerful and so are the decrees you make from that place.

So come on worshipper! Be bold! Let's go!

CHAPTER 5

The Power of Declaration

"In the beginning God created the heavens and the earth. Now the earth was formless and empty, darkness was over the surface of the deep, and the Spirit of God was hovering over the waters. And God said, 'Let there be light,' and there was light." —Genesis 1:1-3 NIV

In the beginning, Scripture says that the Spirit of God hovered over the face of the darkness (Genesis 1:2 NIV). His Spirit was present, hovering, waiting for the spoken word. The Spirit of God wasn't passive—He was poised, ready to respond to God's declaration—yet nothing happened till there was a declaration! *"Let there be light!"*

The Hebrew word *"amar[1]"* used in Genesis implies not just speaking, but declaring with authority and purpose. God's voice wasn't just communicating—it was creating, transforming, and bringing order.

---

1. Biblehub, Strong's Hebrew: 559

God's divine declaration was the catalyst activating the Spirit's creative power. Just like at creation, today, the Spirit of God is poised ready, but now dwelling within us, waiting for powerful declarations that will release His creative and transformative power.

"So shall My word be that goes forth from My mouth; It shall not return to Me void, but it shall accomplish what I please, and it shall prosper in the thing for which I sent it." —Isaiah 55:11 NKJV

For the first six days of creation, God's voice shaped different aspects of creation with both purpose and precision. From the expanse of the heavens to the gathering of waters, from the sprouting of vegetation to the placing of lights in the sky, from the teeming of living creatures to the forming of humankind—each spoken word carried creative power. Each divine declaration brought forth exactly what was commanded and was powerful to achieve exactly what it was sent for. Specific words with specific results. Just as God spoke forth specific words for specific results, we too can be intentional in the words we speak and declare.

The Valley of Dry bones.

"The hand of the Lord was on me, and he brought me out by the Spirit of the Lord and set me in the middle of a valley; it was full of bones." —Ezekiel 37:1 NIV

In one of Scripture's most vivid prophetic encounters, Ezekiel found himself standing in a valley of dry bones. This wasn't just any valley—it was a place where hope had died, where promises lay scattered and broken. The bones were *"very dry"* (Ezekiel 37:2), emphasising their complete lifelessness. Yet in this place of absolute death, God was about to demonstrate the transformative power of prophetic declaration.

In this encounter, God asks Ezekiel a question: *"Son of man, can these bones live?"* (Ezekiel 37:3). This wasn't just a test of Ezekiel's faith—it was an invitation into partnership with divine authority and power. Ezekiel's response to this question reveals both humility and spiritual wisdom: *"Sovereign Lord, you alone know."* In that moment of acknowledged dependence, Ezekiel positioned himself to become a vessel for God's creative word.

What follows next is a masterclass in prophetic declaration. God doesn't simply resurrect the bones Himself—though He certainly could have. Instead, He commands Ezekiel: *"Prophesy to these bones and say to them, 'Dry bones, hear the word of the Lord!'"* (Ezekiel 37:4). Just as in creation when the Spirit hovered waiting for a sound, here too God waited for the prophetic voice of His servant Ezekiel.

"This is what the Sovereign Lord says to these bones: I will make breath enter you, and you will come to life." —Ezekiel 37:5 NIV

Consider the audacity of this moment. Ezekiel is literally speaking to dead, dry bones. To natural ears, this would appear foolish at best, delusional at worst. Yet this is precisely where prophetic declaration operates—in the gap between current reality and God's promised future.

"So I prophesied as I was commanded. And as I was prophesying, there was a noise, a rattling sound, and the bones came together, bone to bone." —Ezekiel 37:7 NIV

The process continues to unfold stage by stage, each declaration bringing a new level of restoration. First came the rattling of bones, then sinews and flesh, until finally the breath of life itself. This progressive restoration teaches us something crucial about prophetic declaration—it often requires sustained proclamation, declaring God's word throughout the process until the full manifestation appears.

The transformation in the valley didn't happen through positive thinking or wishful hoping. It came through specific, authoritative declaration of God's word. Ezekiel didn't just speak generally—he prophesied exactly what God told him to declare. This reminds us that the most powerful declarations are those that align precisely with God's revealed will and purpose.

Like Ezekiel, we too stand in valleys of apparent impossibility. Perhaps it's a family situation that seems beyond hope, a nation that appears to have lost its way, or personal dreams that have long since died. The principle remains the same—when we align our declarations with God's purposes, we partner with His creative power to bring dead things to life.

PRACTICAL APPLICATION

Singing Over Dry Bones

Page 110

The Creative Power of Our Words

If every word spoken from your mouth were to materialise instantly before you—just as God's words did at creation—what would your world look like? Let that question sink in for a moment. Think about the words you've spoken just today: over your family, over your circumstances, in response to challenging news. Now imagine each of those words taking physical form, becoming reality in the space around you. Would you be surrounded by structures of hope and faith, or barriers of doubt and fear?

This isn't just a thought-provoking exercise but a powerful spiritual principle: *"You will also declare a thing, and it will be established for you." —Job 22:28 NKJV*

Most of us have never fully considered the weight our words carry. Yet Scripture states it plainly: *"From the fruit of their mouth a person's stomach is filled; with the harvest of their lips they are satisfied." —Proverbs 18:20 NIV*

Think about that metaphor—we literally eat our own words. Every declaration, every song, every whispered doubt or spoken praise becomes sustenance, not just for us but for those around us. This principle is so potent that Scripture gives us this sobering warning:

"Death and life are in the power of the tongue, and those who love it and indulge it will eat its fruit and bear the consequences of their words." —Proverbs 18:21 AMP

Perhaps this explains David's urgent prayer: *"Set a guard, O Lord, over my mouth; keep watch over the door of my lips!" —Psalm 141:3 NKJV*

He understood something we often forget—our words aren't just expressions of our thoughts; they're creative forces shaping the world around us. As worshippers, each word we speak is like a seed planted in the atmosphere, eventually producing a harvest according to its kind.

From Now On

In 1606 Spanish explorer Pedro Fernandez de Quiros navigated his way onto Australian shores and declared these powerful words:

"Let the heavens, the earth, the waters with all their creatures and all those here present witness that I, Captain Pedro Fernandez de Quiros, in the name of Jesus Christ, hoist this emblem of the Holy Cross on which Jesus Christ's person was crucified and whereon He gave His life for the ransom and remedy of the human race, on this day of Pentecost, 14 May 1606, I take possession of all this part of the South as far as the pole in the name of Jesus, which from now on shall be called the Southern land of the Holy Spirit and this always and forever to the end that to all natives, in all the said lands, the holy, sacred evangel may be preached zealously and openly."

These words weren't just a colonial proclamation, but a prophetic declaration that would define the identity and destiny of the entire nation of Australia. The power of this declaration still resonates today, as Australia continues to be known as *"The Great Southland of the Holy Spirit."*

Immortalised in the Song, *"The Great Southland[2]"* released in 1993 by Geoff Bullock, these words quickly have become a powerful declaration, burning Heaven's decree into the hearts and the lips of the people.

Today, God is calling His worshipping army to arise with

---

2. The Great Southland © 1993 Geoff Bullock Music

similar boldness. He's looking for those who will make bold and powerful "from now on" declarations that will redirect the course of our nation. Not just hopeful wishes or positive confessions—but prophetic statements aligned with Heaven's purposes.

Stifling the Voice of Doubt & Unbelief

In this season of taking ground, there is no room for unbelief and doubt as this will directly come against what God wants to do. Consider the example of Jesus. Scripture tells us He could do no mighty works in His own hometown because of unbelief.

"Now He could do no mighty work there, except that He laid His hands on a few sick people and healed them. And He marveled because of their unbelief." —Mark 6:5-6 NKJV

The same Jesus who calmed storms and raised the dead found His ministry influence and impact extremely limited. This wasn't a representation of Jesus' lack of power—it was a demonstration of how unbelief can hinder us from receiving from the promise from Heaven.

As worshippers in this season our belief system needs to align with the belief system of Heaven—not our own experiences or understandings defined by human perspectives. There is more required of us. We are called to be people of faith. We need to shut the mouth of unbelief.

Zechariah

In Luke 1, the angel Gabriel tells Zechariah that God has heard his prayers and that his wife Elizabeth would bear him a son! Full of doubt and unbelief, Zechariah responds to the message with *"How shall I know this? For I am an old man, and my wife is well advanced in years" (vs 18).* Due to his unbelief the angel shut Zechariah's mouth, leaving him unable to speak for the duration of the pregnancy, only undoing this when the promise had been fulfilled. So potent was the power of Zechariah's doubt and unbelief that it was deemed better to seal his lips, than contradict the promise of Heaven. A lesson for us that if we cannot speak in faith and in agreement with what Heaven is saying, then it is better for us not to speak at all!

Our Responsibility

Today, for worshippers, leaders and prophetic voices, we are called to live by a higher standard. Our words carry weight in the spirit realm, making our faith—or lack thereof—a potent force. Every time we worship, sing, write songs, or make declarations, we have the opportunity to intentionally come against doubt and build faith! Bold faith and powerful declarations are what we need in this time to step into what God wants to do.

"You will also declare a thing, And it will be established for you." –Job 22:28 NKJV

Scripture is clear: the words WE speak matter significantly. They do, however, need to be aligned with God's will, His heart, and intentions to be effective. It is important to note that we cannot simply manifest whatever our heart desires because of the words we speak.

What Scripture Says

Scripture consistently speaks about the power of our words. Here are some powerful scriptural examples.

- **Words are a tree of life, or breaker of the spirit**
  Proverbs 15:4 NKJV: "A wholesome tongue is a tree of life, But perverseness in it breaks the spirit."

- **Words have the power to bring life or death**
  Proverbs 18:21 NIV: "The tongue has the power of life and death, and those who love it will eat its fruit."

- **Our tongues can bless or curse**
  James 3:9-10 NIV: "With the tongue we praise our Lord and Father, and with it we curse human beings, who have been made in God's likeness. Out of the same mouth comes praise and cursing. My brothers and sisters, this should not be."

- **Words created the universe**
  Hebrews 11:3 NIV: "By faith, we understand that the

universe was formed at God's command so that what is seen was not made out of what was visible."
Genesis 1:3 NIV: "And God said, 'Let there be light,' and there was light."

- **Can calm storms**
Mark 4:39 NKJV: Jesus demonstrated the power of His spoken word when He calmed the storm with a simple command, "Peace, be still"

- **Words have emotional & physical impact on the body**
Proverbs 16:24 NIV: "Gracious words are a honeycomb, sweet to the soul and healing to the bones."

- **Words can bring healing**
Psalm 107:20 NIV: "He sent out his word and healed them; he rescued them from the grave".

- **Words can raise the dead**
John 11:43 NKJV: "When he had said this, Jesus called in a loud voice, "Lazarus, come out!" The dead man came out, his hands and feet wrapped with strips of linen, and a cloth around his face".

- **We will yield the results of our words**
Proverbs 18:20 NIV: "From the fruit of their mouth a person's stomach is filled; with the harvest of their lips, they are satisfied."

- **Can move mountains**
  Mark 11:22-24 NIV: "Have faith in God," Jesus answered. "Truly I tell you, if anyone says to this mountain, 'Go, throw yourself into the sea,' and does not doubt in their heart but believes that what they say will happen, it will be done for them. Therefore I tell you, whatever you ask for in prayer, believe that you have received it, and it will be yours."

- **The word builds faith**
  Romans 10:17 NKJV. "So then faith comes by hearing, and hearing by the word of God."

Building Unshakeable Faith

Are you convinced yet? As we move into seasons of increased spiritual warfare it becomes more and more neccesary to step into higher levels of faith. We can no longer afford casual doubt or flippant unbelief. The stakes are too high. Just as Joshua and Caleb's faith-filled report stood against the doubt of ten other spies, our declarations must also maintain faith regardless of circumstances.

The antidote to doubt isn't wishful thinking or blind optimism—it's built on the solid foundation of God's word.

"Faith comes by hearing, and hearing by the word of God". – Romans 10:17 NKJV.

We must intentionally saturate ourselves in the word of God until faith becomes our default response and we become bold giants of faith, unshakable in any situation.

Worship Leaders & Songwriters

For worship leaders and songwriters, this understanding yields very practical implications, because it is us who often take on the responsibility of presenting the word before our people through our songs. Every week we have the opportunity to build our people into giants of the faith, taking them into higher levels of their walk with the Lord. We need to become the theologians who rightfully present the word to our people. It is therefore of utmost importance that:

- *Our lyrics be saturated with Scripture*
- *Our declarations align with God's promises*
- *Our testimonies must reinforce faith*
- *Our conversations must build expectancy*
- *Our responses to challenges must demonstrate faith*

I believe we need to stop singing songs that cater to our emotions and earthly experiences, and use our songs strategically to build greater faith and expectancy into God's people and advance the kingdom.

The Sound of Faith in Adversary

As believers, we must become people of unstoppable faith even in the midst of great adversity. We must become like those in the book of Acts, who while facing great trial and persecution, didn't voice doubt or fear—but continued to lift their voices in faith-filled declaration (Acts 4:24-31). Their response literally shook their gathering place and resulted in increased boldness and miraculous demonstrations of God's power. When trouble came, they praised and worshipped even more fervently.

PRACTICAL APPLICATION

The Power of Declaration

Page 112

Let this be our model. Every song, every declaration and every faith filled expression must reinforce trust in God's character and confidence in His promises. The world is depending on us for it. This nation is depending on us for it.

CHAPTER 6

The Prophetic Sound of David's Tabernacle

When we look for a model of authentic worship, our eyes turn to King David—a man after God's own heart, who penned most of the Psalms and exemplified what it means to be a true worshipper. The establishment of his tabernacle became a divine blueprint that still shapes how we approach worship today. In implementing the tabernacle, David appointed three key leaders, along with their decendants, whose approach to worship significantly impacted not only the nation of their time but also the way we understand worship today.

"Moreover David and the captains of the army separated for the service some of the sons of Asaph, of Heman, and of Jeduthun, who should prophesy with harps, stringed instruments, and cymbals." – 1 Chronicles 25:1 NKJV

Let's examine this. Firstly, David chose those *"who should prophesy with harps, stringed instruments, and cymbals."* Notice that their primary role was to prophesy—not to play music. Music was only mentioned secondarily as the means by which they would prophesy.

The word *"prophesy"* comes from the Hebrew root word *'naba'*[1], meaning to speak by divine inspiration. The ability to hear God's voice and bring forth His word, messages, and strategies was David's first priority within the temple, and it should be ours as well. The outworking of this in the context of our worship practice today is what we have come to know as *"prophetic worship"*.

All three appointed leaders were not only skilled musicians but also recognised as seers. Asaph was known as *"Asaph the Seer"* (2 Chronicles 29:30), Heman as *"the king's seer in the words of God"* (1 Chronicles 25:5), and while Jeduthun isn't explicitly called a seer, he was set apart for *"prophesying with the harp."* Their role was to receive Heaven's messages and strategies, then translate them into sounds and songs that would guide and strengthen God's people.

This is what we should aspire to be—conduits of Heaven's messages and strategies through our sound and song, not merely providers of music or entertainment.

The Nature of David's Prophetic Songs

The nature of the prophetic songs written and brought forth by David and the other writers of the tabernacle varied in theme and

---

1. BibleHub, Strong's Hebrew: 5012

expression and were brought forth to encourage, build and edify the nation and it's people. Themes included:

- **Songs of corporate gathering and worship**
  Their songs unified the people of Israel in praising God together, fostering community and communal reverence for His presence.

  "Oh, magnify the LORD with me, and let us exalt His name together. " –Psalm 34:3 NKJV

  "Make a joyful shout to the LORD, all you lands! Serve the LORD with gladness; come before His presence with singing –Psalm 100:1-2 NKJV

- **Songs of personal worship**
  These songs expressed individual devotion, gratitude, or lament, allowing worshippers to engage deeply with God on a personal level.

  "Bless the LORD, O my soul; and all that is within me, bless His holy name!" –Psalm 103:1 NKJV

  "As the deer pants for the water brooks, so pants my soul for You, O God. –Psalm 42:1 NKJV

- **Songs of prophetic encouragement to the people**
Songs that reminded Israel of God's faithfulness and power, encouraging them to trust in Him during trials.

"Wait on the LORD; be of good courage, and He shall strengthen your heart; wait, I say, on the LORD!" –Psalm 27:14 NKJV

- **Songs of prophetic warning to the people**
These psalms admonished Israel to remain faithful to God and avoid the consequences of sin and disobedience.

"Today, if you will hear His voice: 'Do not harden your hearts, as in the rebellion.'" –Psalm 95:7-8 NKJV

"For the LORD knows the way of the righteous, but the way of the ungodly shall perish." –Psalm 1:6 NKJV

- **Messianic prophecy**
Beyond encouragement, many psalms contained prophetic declarations, pointing to Jesus Christ.

"The LORD said to my Lord, Sit at My right hand, till I make Your enemies Your footstool. –Psalm 110:1 NKJV

"My God, My God, why have You forsaken Me?" –Psalm 22:1 NKJV, foreshadowing Christ's suffering.

> "I will open my mouth in a parable; I will utter dark sayings of old." –Psalm 78:2 NKJV

The songs penned by David's Psalmists were never for entertainment's sake. They were powerful communicators of the Kingdom of Heaven to God's people. Today, as worshippers we can learn from the songs they wrote and understand that the most powerful songs we could bring are the ones inspired by the Holy Spirit.

Stewards of the Presence

The impact of Asaph, Heman, and Jeduthun extended far beyond their personal ministries in David's Tabernacle. These three seers were also entrusted with a greater mandate: raising up a company of prophetic worshippers who would carry their mantle. This wasn't a small undertaking—together they trained 288 others, including their own children, creating a generational legacy of prophetic sound which continued for generations to come. These three worship leaders and their families faithfully served not only under King David's leadership and vision, but continued their priesthood into the reign of David's son Solomon.

The undeniable impact of their worship is seen in many areas, however, perhaps one of the most glorious stories can be seen in the dedication of Solomon's temple.

"All the Levites who were musicians-Asaph, Heman, Jeduthun and their sons and relatives-stood on the east side of the altar, dressed in fine linen and playing cymbals, harps and lyres. They were accompanied by 120 priests sounding trumpets. The trumpeters and musicians joined in unison to give praise and thanks to the LORD. Accompanied by trumpets, cymbals and other instruments, the singers raised their voices in praise to the LORD and sang: "He is good; his love endures forever." Then the temple of the LORD was filled with the cloud, and the priests could not perform their service because of the cloud, for the glory of the LORD filled the temple of God." –2 Chronicles 5:12-14 NKJV

What a monumental occasion that was not only a religious event, but one that was significant in the history of the nation. The worshippers who served during this occasion were not only skilled, but through their worship provided a dwelling place for the manifest presence of God. Their worship was so acceptable to Him, that He came with the full approval of his presence. So strong was the Glory that those who served were all unable to continue to do so.

The fact that the Glory of the Lord came and filled Solomon's temple wasn't just a chance occurrence but was undoubtedly a culmination of decades of disciplined training, devoted worship, and prophetic sensitivity cultivated within David's tabernacle.

Could you imagine if the same thing happened today? If the

dedication of a building in our nation's capital called upon the worshippers to minister and the presence of the Lord became so thick that no one could stand? Could you imagine how the nation would respond? I believe the days where the manifest presence of God is coming in greater measure and will be seen by many, just as it was at that time.

As worshippers, should we wish to see the same, where the Glory of God rests upon the throne of our worship, we cannot rely on the latest formula, hit song or church strategy. We must grab hold of only those things that carry an eternal significance and live lives of consecration, servanthood and develop deeper intimacy with the Holy Spirit. I believe that only when the Holy Spirit can rest on the throne of our own personal worship, can we expect to see him move in the greater context of the nation.

Worship Warriors

Another of David's fundamental considerations when it came to choosing Asaph, Heman and Jeduthun as temple leaders, was the consideration of worship as a weapon of national warfare.

"Moreover David and the captains of the army separated for the service some of the sons of Asaph, of Heman, and of Jeduthun."
–1 Chronicles 25:1

It was not just King David who had input into the choosing of his chief worshippers, but the leaders of the army also. This wasn't just a casual arrangement giving musicians a platform to encourage or entertain. No! It was a strategic placement of spiritual warriors designed for maximum impact in warfare.

David and the military leaders ultimately understood and had faith in the power of worship, recognising it as an essential military strategy. It was about deploying spiritual weapons with precision and purpose.

We see a powerful outworking of this military strategy approximately 100 years later in 2 Chronicles chapter 20 where Jehoshaphat draws upon the strategic wisdom established generations earlier, making what must have seemed an outrageous military decision to many:

"After consulting the people, Jehoshaphat appointed men to sing to the Lord and to praise him for the splendor of his holiness as they went out at the head of the army, saying: 'Give thanks to the Lord, for his love endures forever.' As they began to sing and praise, the Lord set ambushes against the men of Ammon and Moab and Mount Seir who were invading Judah, and they were defeated. The Ammonites and Moabites rose up against the men from Mount Seir to destroy and annihilate them. After they finished slaughtering the men from Seir, they helped to destroy one another." –2 Chronicles 20:21-23 NIV

Jehoshaphat positions the worshippers at the front of the army - not the back - the front. Imagine that! Even ahead of the weaponry and those trained in deadly combat. In the natural world this strategy would have seemed like utter foolishness, but was one that secured a victorious outcome for the entire nation, changing its entire destiny.

This battle strategy was not simply a historical tale - but is to be a true testament to the power of worship in spiritual warfare and an example for us today.

Today as we look face-to-face at many enemies that would come against us, God has made it clear - that our eyes must be on Jesus, and that worship must become a weapon of choice.

The question is not if the weapons and strategies of worship as warfare work - they do - but are we bold enough, or even motivated enough, to engage in the battle in the first place.

That All Would Prophesy

The model of prophetic worship that David established wasn't just an Old Testament story to be admired from a generational distance—It was an example of how we as worshippers can prophetically bring forth songs that encourage, edify and give direction to a nation.

This prophetic nature in worship is something we should be seeing more of these days. Why? Because scripture says so:

*"I will pour out my Spirit on **all** flesh; your sons and your daughters shall prophesy." –Joel 2:28 NKJV*

This promise, now realised through the indwelling Holy Spirit, means every born-again believer carries the capacity to hear and release Heaven's sound. Every believer now has the ability to worship prophetically in the same way as David's mighty worshippers and with presumably the same results.

When we speak of restoring David's Tabernacle—a phrase often heard in modern worship circles—we're not calling for a historical reenactment. We are addressing the need to rediscover our role as vessels of Heaven's sound, embracing a lifestyle of prophetic worship that ushers in God's glory, determines the outcome of warfare, and shifts the direction of a nation.

This prophetic dimension of worship isn't reserved for a select few who hold platform positions or possess exceptional talent. It's the birthright of every Spirit-filled believer—all who are called to worship in Spirit and truth.

In this critical hour, God is raising up prophetic worshippers who understand both the privilege and responsibility of releasing Heaven's sound on behalf of the nation. These aren't just musicians or singers—they're ministers of His presence, stewards of His purposes, and catalysts for breakthrough. Through their yielded lives and voices, Heaven's reality breaks into Earth's atmosphere, preparing the way for the greatest outpouring of God's Spirit this world has ever seen.

Restoring the Prophetic Sound

Restoring the prophetic sound is not a return to an old model, but a reawakening of Heaven's original intent for worship. To restore this prophetic sound, we must embrace a number of things with intentionality including:

- **Cultivating Intimacy with God**
  Prophetic worship flows from a place of deep intimacy. We can only release what we've first received from God. Like David and his worshippers, we must prioritise time in His presence, seek to know His heart and hear His voice. Worshippers must be devoted to prayer, scripture, and personal worship, allowing the Holy Spirit to shape the sound they will ultimately release.

- **We Must Be Priests**
  Just as David's mighty worshippers acted as priests bridging the gap between God and man—we must also. Our worship must be done, for the people; on behalf of

the people. Our worship must direct the peoples' attention towards God, and then in turn deliver God's message to his people.

- **Train and Disciple Prophetic Worshippers**
  Just as Asaph, Heman, and Jeduthun raised up a company of worshippers, we too must invest in equipping ourselves, as well as equipping and mentoring others. This involves nurturing spiritual maturity, musical skill, and the ability to discern and respond to God's leading. It's not enough to be talented; worshippers must also be spiritually grounded.

PRACTICAL APPLICATION

Worshippers as Priests

Page 114

As we cultivate intimacy, embrace our priestly identity, and train others to carry the weight of prophetic responsibility, we position ourselves to release a sound that carries God's heart, transforms lives, and shifts the atmosphere wherever it's heard. It is a sound that must be released if we want to see a shift in our nation and the nations.

CHAPTER 7

Hearing Heaven: Discerning God's Voice for the Prophetic Sound

Jesus: Our Example

"I no longer call you servants," Jesus declared, *"because a servant does not know his master's business. Instead, I have called you friends, for everything that I learned from my Father I have made known to you." –John 15:15 NIV*

This remarkable shift from servants to friends carries great implications for worshippers and prophetic voices in the church today.

Jesus established a pattern of paternership with the Father that we are called to emulate when he said *"I must be about my Father's business"* (Luke 2:49). This revealed a life aligned with Heaven's agenda. Later, He would affirm this fact, *"For I did not speak on my own, but the Father who sent me commanded me to say all that I have spoken"* (John 12:49). This wasn't mere obedience—it was intimate partnership with Heaven - one that brought about the miraculous.

Jesus' authority flowed from this alignment. Every miracle, every breakthrough, every transformation came because He spoke what He heard the Father say. The same is available for us today with the indwelling, ever present Holy Spirit. The gift of the Holy Spirit is all the equipping we need to fulfill the greatest mission there ever was - the great commission.

"Go therefore and make disciples of all the nations, baptising them in the name of the Father and of the Son and of the Holy Spirit, teaching them to observe all things that I have commanded you; and lo, I am with you always, even to the end of the age." Amen. –Matthew 28:19-20 NKJV

On this mission we are now invited to follow Jesus' model and go in his name, saying the things that He tells us to say. We are now His mouthpieces on the earth.

Imagine the impact on our churches, homes, and cities if we, like Jesus, only released the sounds and declarations we heard from the Father. This would no doubt transform every sphere— family, government, education, everywhere — because God's word never returns void (Isaiah 55:11).

This is a powerful invitation, one that every worshipper needs to accept. To become co-labourers with Christ and to actively listen and replicate God's words on the earth–not ours. Not only in our speech, but in our sound and songs also.

The Sound for the Season

Just like Jesus, we too must be timely in the words we speak and also in the songs we sing. Heaven is always speaking, always releasing fresh sounds and songs for each moment and season.

The question isn't whether God is speaking—it's whether we're positioned to listen and bold enough to release what we hear - just like the story I shared about the backing vocalist and the war cry.

As worshippers and prophetic voices, we carry the responsibility of not just making music and song, but of releasing the *"now"* sounds that transform atmospheres, establish kingdom, and prepare the way for breakthrough.

Just as God declares, *"Behold, I am doing a new thing; do you not perceive it?"* (Isaiah 43:19), we must develop sensitivity to perceive the sound of each season. This isn't just about hearing— it's about discernment.

The Sons of Issachar exemplified this in David's time; they

"understood the times and knew what Israel should do" (1 Chronicles 12:32). These men were invaluable to David's army because they could discern not just what was happening, but what was needed for that particular moment. They were able to bring Heaven's wisdom and strategy. We too must do the same.

PRACTICAL APPLICATION

Tuning in to His Voice

Page 116

Today, we must ask ourselves: What is God doing in this moment? What declaration is Heaven waiting to partner with? What sound will break open this season of revival we're contending for? In our homes? In our regions? In the nation?

When we align our sounds with Heaven's voice, we become catalysts for transformation. Our songs become more than music—they become weapons that establish Heaven's reality on Earth. In this critical hour, may we have ears to hear what the Spirit is saying and courage to release the sound of Heaven for our time.

So how do we hear and recognise the times, seasons and the songs and declarations we should be making? Well, Heaven's voice reaches us through multiple channels, each vital for releasing the right sound in the right seasons

The Living Word

God's kingdom is established through His word. Scripture isn't just ancient text—it's *"God-breathed"* (2 Timothy 3:16) and *"living and powerful"* (Hebrews 4:12). When we sing and declare the word, we partner with the living nature of Scripture, meaning verses written thousands of years ago carry the same creative power today as when they were first written and spoken.

This is why theological accuracy in our worship songs isn't optional—it's essential. Every declaration of Scripture carries the power to perform itself, establishing the very reality it describes. When we sing about God's healing, those very words carry healing power. When we declare His promises of provision, those words begin creating that reality. When we proclaim His victory, those declarations carry the same authority that split the Red Sea and brought down Jericho's walls.

If you are ever unsure what the Lord would be saying over a situation, go to the word where His promises are only good and perfect. The Bible isn't just a reference book—it's a creative force waiting to be released through aligned declaration. God has already provided His perspective and promise for every situation we face. Whether you're dealing with fear, sickness, lack, or any other challenge, Scripture contains the creative declaration needed for breakthrough. We just need to partner with it.

This understanding should also revolutionise how we approach songwriting and worship leading. Our songs shouldn't just quote Scripture—they should release its creative power.

Remember, Isaiah 55:11 promises that God's word never returns void but accomplishes everything He sends it to do. When we align our worship with Scripture, we're partnering with this unstoppable creative force. Let the word of God be your first and primary source for prophetic declaration, knowing that Heaven's power is already resident within its promises.

The Voice of our Leaders

As worshippers, we must also align with those charged with shepherding God's people and leading us in our various missions. Our pastors and leaders spend hours in prayer and study, seeking God's direction for this season. Their messages aren't merely sermons—they're prophetic declarations of Heaven's current agenda for their regions, missions and their people—or at least they should be. When we engage with and amplify these messages through songs and declaration, we turn the language of Heaven into the songs of the people.

Doing this effectively requires developing relationships with leaders and spiritual sensitivity to recognise the prophetic threads woven through their messages. Often, a single phrase or declaration from the pulpit carries a seed of something Heaven wants to establish in the people. As worshippers and even songwriters, we have the unique opportunity to water these seeds through song, helping them take root in the hearts of God's people.

Remember, transformation only truly happens when truth moves from the head to the heart, and one of the most potent ways for this to happen is through the songs we sing.

PRACTICAL APPLICATION

Sermons Into Songs

Page 118

Just as the Levites worked in harmony with the priests in the temple, today's worship leaders must work in harmony with pastoral leadership. This doesn't stifle creativity—it focuses it. When we understand the current emphasis of Heaven for our own churches, we can channel our creative energy into songs that will have maximum kingdom impact far beyond our own church's walls. From Jerusalem, to Judea and Samaria to the ends of the earth!

The Voice of the Prophets

Just as we align with pastoral leadership and ground ourselves in Scripture, we must also attune our ears to what God is saying through His seasoned prophetic voices. Throughout history, God has used prophets to declare His plans and purposes over nations and regions. These words, when properly discerned and embraced, become catalysts for transformation.

Prophetic words released over our nation and regions aren't just encouraging messages—they're blueprints for breakthrough. When God speaks through trusted prophetic voices, He's inviting us to partner with Him to see them established on the Earth. Consider how many prophetic words have been spoken over Australia about revival, about being the Great Southland of the Holy Spirit, about a youth awakening. These aren't just nice ideas; they're Heaven's intentions waiting for Earth's agreement and activation. We must, however, actively partner with Him if we want to see them come to pass.

One of the best ways to partner with these prophetic words is through the songs we write and sing. When we craft songs that capture the essence of prophetic declarations, we provide God's people with tools to agree with Heaven's purposes. These songs help prophetic words move from mental understanding to heart-level faith and expectation.

Consider how many of David's psalms (songs) carried prophetic revelation about the coming Messiah, building faith and expectation, generations before Christ was born. David took what God was revealing and turned it into songs that Israel could carry for generations, all until they saw the fulfillment of the promise.

In the same way, we can take the prophetic words spoken over our nation and craft them into declarations that build faith. Doing so creates an opportunity for the wider body to actively engage and contend for the fulfilment of those prophetic words.

PRACTICAL APPLICATION

Partnering with Prophetic Words

Page 120

However, this isn't just about writing songs—it's about actively participating in creating *all* the conditions for prophetic fulfilment. If there's a word about youth revival, we might need to create more opportunities for young people to lead in worship. If there's a declaration about unity in the body of Christ, we might need to initiate collaborative worship gatherings across denominational lines. Partnership with God's agenda is strategic and often we need to create the structures where the prophetic sound and declaration can be released.

The Power of a Personal Song

God often speaks personally to each of us, providing unique songs, and sounds for every season and moment of our lives. These revelations often come in unexpected ways—perhaps through a melody that awakens us in the night, a phrase that captures the heart during personal worship, or a scripture that suddenly comes with fresh revelation. Lean into these songs. Sometimes His Spirit will bring to remembrance a song that, when sung, will bring healing or comfort in a certain area, or will build faith and expectancy in another. Sometimes it may require you to write your own song led by the Holy Spirit's prompting. For whatever reason His Spirit breathes on a song, if Heaven inspired, it carries Heaven's purpose.

My Own Song

A few years ago, I remember a season when I was having trouble sleeping. I would find myself waking in the middle of the night anxious and worried about things I was unable to control. It ended up impacting every area of my life. In an effort to intentionally shift my situation I went to my bible and my intentional meditation became this verse.

"Be anxious for nothing, but in everything by prayer and supplication, with thanksgiving, let your requests be made known to God; and the peace of God, which surpasses all understanding, will guard your hearts and minds through Christ Jesus." – Philipians 4:6-7 KNJV

This scripture was something I turned into a song–one I would sing over myself daily. I sung it over myself as I prepared myself for bed, as I got ready for work and during times I was feeling particularly anxious. I did this for months until one day I realised that I had been sleeping through the night completely free from fear and anxiety, despite the circumstances not being any different. I realised I was now walking (or should I say sleeping) in the fulfillment of the words I had been singing over myself - *"I will be anxious for nothing"*. It was a powerful personal revelation of the power of a personal song that brought personal breakthrough.

While sometimes personal songs are for our own personal edification and encouragement, sometimes they become an assignment or an opportunity. Something God can use to reach and impact others who are going through the same season.

The Song for the Moment

Sometimes the Lord will breathe on a particular song for a moment or a season, which may be used to do things such as build faith or bring comfort.

I remember one particular incidence of this when I was asked to sing at a funeral which was attended mostly by non-believers. The song *"Amazing Grace"* was a song that was bringing me great comfort in that season as I too processed the emotions of loss. The song was not just a song of comfort for me, but I saw it as an opportunity to publicly proclaim and release God's *"Amazing Grace"* over the people as they mourned. As I stood and sang that song, I did so with the intentionality of releasing God's grace over the people. After the ceremony, many people approached me and told me how impacted they were. Some even made commented that they *"could feel it"*. They could feel the anointing which had ministered to them. That particular song was not just a song but an opportunity for an encounter in the midst of difficult circumstances.

Writing the Songs for Tomorrow

I love it how Pastor Bill Johnson from Bethel Church puts it. In challenging his team to consider where they want to see the church in 20 years, he told them *"Write the songs about it now, and we'll sing our way into it"*[1]. Wow! A powerful prophetic and pre-emptive approach to worship. What do we want to see in 20 years? Where do we want to see our nation in the future? Well we had better start writing the songs now! This challenge places such a weighty responsibility on songwriters to write the songs that will carry the nation forward into the divinely appointed things of God.

PRACTICAL APPLICATION

Writing the Songs for Tomorrow

Page 122

Writing these songs, however, must have one major consideration if we are to see the full impact. We must be deliberate in the words we write and sing. Our lyrical content matters. I believe we need to move away from songs that speak simply to our own human

---

1 Bill Johnson, Facebook post, March 14, 2025, https://www.facebook.com/BillJohnsonMinistries/photos/1161472978679226.

experience and into songs that carry the weight of the kingdom. Songs that are prophetically inspired like those written by David and his leaders of worship. Songs that speak of God's majesty, His glory and present the truth of how great He truly is.

Our songs must also be theologically sound carying the weight and the truth of scripture. Charles Wesley wrote 8,989 hymns[2] during the course of his lifetime, with many being during the first great awakening. These songs were written predominantly so the people would learn theological truths and ultimately be changed as they encountered the truth of the word of God, presented through song.

It is time for us as worshippers to become more intentional with the songs we sing and write. There is no point in writing and singing songs for the sake of entertainment. Entertainment might draw a crowd, but only the anointing and an encounter with the living God can truly transform lives.

Our songs must carry the anointing of God if it is to change atmospheres over our homes and regions, release faith and expectancy and facilitate genuine encounters with God. Anointing can only come from consecration, intimacy and intentionality when it comes to doing the Father's will.

---

2 "Golden Age of Hymns: Did You Know?" Christian History Institute. Accessed March 14, 2025. https://christianhistoryinstitute.org/magazine/article/golden-age-of-hymns-did-you-know.

In what ever way we bring forth the new prophetic song, now is the time! Now is the time to bring forth the songs that will carry the next move of God to the nation!

Come on worshipper - release the songs and sounds that will impact the nation!

CHAPTER 8

The Call to Unity: One Sound - Many voices

I believe the weight of what the Lord wants to do in this nation is so huge that it cannot be sustained by one group alone. It must be a collective effort, where the body unifies in order to build His earthly place of habitation. If we are truly going to see a mighty move of God, there's one principle we must grasp with both hands: unity. Not the superficial unity of simple agreement, but the unity that releases heaven's power.

This concept of unity is one that is so foundational that Scripture tells us we need to have our unity in order *before* we even approach worship.

In Matthew 5:23-24, Jesus himself said *"Therefore if you bring your gift to the altar, and there remember that your brother has something against you, leave your gift there before the altar, and go your way. First be reconciled to your brother, and then come and offer your gift.*

Unity is not something that we can simply push aside for convenience sake. So what does this unity look like?

The Oxford Dictionary defines unity as *"the state of being united or joined as a whole."* Yet God's version of unity goes beyond this: it's not about uniformity, but harmony; not about sameness, but synchronised purpose.

Picture a grand symphony orchestra. Each instrument carries its distinct voice—the mellow warmth of woodwinds, the bright clarity of brass, the rich resonance of strings. If every instrument had the same tone or played the same note, we'd lose the masterpiece the composer envisioned. The power lies not in uniformity but in diversity working together in perfect harmony. This is God's blueprint for His church. Empowered individuals, as God's instruments that make a unique sound when he works through us. When those sounds are all played together, what a glorious sound we will make!

Romans 12:5-6 says: *"For just as each of us has one body with many members, and these members do not all have the same function, so in Christ we, though many, form one body, and each member belongs to all the others."* NIV

One body, many members, different functions—yet all essential to the whole. When we understand this, we begin to see that our differences aren't obstacles to overcome but instruments to harmonise.

When Jesus returns, He's not coming for a fragmented bride divided by denominational lines. He's not seeking the Baptist bride, the Pentecostal bride, or the Catholic bride. He's coming for His unified church. The church therefore must grasp this truth: our unity is not an option; it's essential for the coming move of God.

The understanding of this truth ultimately demands intentional action. We must deliberately lay aside the things that divide, reaching beyond the comfortable walls of our own congregations, ministries, and denominations. As Psalm 133 declares, *"How good and pleasant it is when God's people live together in unity... for there the Lord bestows his blessing."* There it is... it's about ALL God's people. Unity creates an atmosphere where God's blessing isn't just requested—it's commanded.

The Song That Unifies

One day in a moment of curiosity and contemplation, I was meditating on why the Lord chose music and song as a preferred method of corporate praise and worship. What He dropped in my heart was simple and profound: *"Where there is a song, there is unity."*

This truth becomes evident when you look at the context of any gathering of believers, each member coming with their own unique background, perspectives, baggage, and each with a unique sound and expression. The complex mixture of individualities makes it difficult for unity.

Here is an example: If I were to give the instruction to a group of people to *"Praise the Lord"* without any further instruction, we would find that the responses could vary widely. Some may bow in reverence, others sing loudly, while some might dance enthusiastically. This would depend on many things including their denominational experience, their giftings, preferred means of personal expression and even the influences of their own churches. Each expression is valid, yet diverse. If this diversity is not handled well then the gathering as a whole would lack unity. How then do we create unity from such differences? Give them a song!

If we were to take a different approach and say to the congregation, *"Let's all sing Amazing Grace together,"* something beautiful happens. Every voice finds its place in the melody, every heart aligns with words that are being spoken, and suddenly, the many become one voice in praising the Lord. This isn't only just about musical synchronisation; it's about hearts beating in unified purpose, the people building their faith and expectation together and becoming an integral part of something greater than themselves.

We see this power of musical unity demonstrated daily in stadiums, at celebrations, and in gatherings worldwide. If secular music can create such camaraderie and a powerful atmosphere that echoes throughout the streets, how much more powerful is the sound of combined voices in worship—one the world needs to hear.

We've already looked at this but let's look at it again with a different lens. In 2 Chronicles 5:13 we read:

"Indeed it came to pass, when the trumpeters and singers were as one, to make one sound to be heard in praising and thanking the LORD, and when they lifted up their voice with the trumpets and cymbals and instruments of music, and praised the LORD, saying: 'For He is good, For His mercy endures forever,' that the house, the house of the LORD, was filled with a cloud." NKJV

Diversity of sounds and expressions together in a harmonised and synchronised sound of praise is something so beautiful that the presence of God came and rested on the people. It wasn't just a song that created this dynamic but the unified hearts of the people in awe and reverence singing in one accord. The unification of the people. Perfect harmony and perfect unity.

Can I encourage you, do not underestimate the power of the song in establishing a place of unity and blessing in your homes, churches and the regions. If you want unity, start with a song.

Unity of the Spirit

A.W. Tozer captured this principle beautifully when he observed that one hundred pianos tuned to the same fork are automatically tuned to each other. They achieve harmony not by focusing on one another, but by each aligning with a higher standard. Similarly, when worshippers fix their gaze on Christ rather than becoming preoccupied with the things that divide, or even the concept of trying to attain unity itself, they find themselves drawn into supernatural alignment and ultimately, unity.

During a recent conversation, a friend shared a profound insight with me about achieving true unity: *"If we really want unity, the only true way is if we teach every person to hear from the Holy Spirit for themselves."* It's so true! Unity isn't achieved through external means but through every worshipper's internal alignment with the Spirit's leading.

PRACTICAL APPLICATION

The Sound of Unity

Page 124

When every believer is tuned to the Holy Spirit, unity becomes the natural outcome. Discord often stems from prioritising personal agendas and individual interpretations over the Spirit's leading. This doesn't mean abandoning our distinct beliefs or expressions—rather, it means holding them in proper tension with the greater purpose of kingdom advancement.

Unity for the Sake of Revival

How badly do you want to see the Spirit of God move in this nation, in your home and regions? How badly do you want revival? I believe that now is the time, and as Australia stands on the brink of a great outpouring, the call to unity becomes increasingly urgent. We must move beyond theoretical agreement to practical demonstration. We must be purposeful. When we worship together, pray together, and pursue God's purposes together, we create an atmosphere where Heaven's sound can resonate without hindrance. The breakthroughs we seek—in our families, communities, and nation—await our unified response to heaven's invitation.

Unity is costly. Are we willing to pay the price for it? Will we lay aside personal preferences for corporate purpose? Will we value diversity while pursuing harmony? The sound of breakthrough we long to hear may well depend on how we answer these questions.

CHAPTER 9

Your Voice - Your Territory

Every worshipper carries a unique sound from heaven—an expression that, when released in its proper context, creates a powerful breakthrough. Yet one of the greatest challenges many worshippers face is misunderstanding the nature of their gifting, often measuring success solely by platform ministry as the measuring stick. This limited perspective has led many into disappointment when their expression of worship is not done in the way they think it should.

"For just as we have many members in one body and all the members do not have the same function, so we, who are many, are one body in Christ, and individually members one of another. Since we have gifts that differ according to the grace given to us, each of us is to exercise them accordingly ..." –Romans 12:4-6 NASB

This was something that the Lord highlighted to me in a powerful way during a 24-hour worship gathering we had arranged to coincide with our national election. During this gathering, rather than focusing on politics or other societal issues, we simply felt called to exalt Jesus over the nation—so that's what we did! It was a powerful weekend.

During this time, part of what unfolded was a beautiful demonstration of how various worship gifts operate in their divine assignments.

I led the opening session for the weekend, alongside an incredibly anointed violinist. This session carried a particular prophetic edge, which was very much the expression of both of our gifts combined. The room was engaged and the atmosphere was charged with expectation. After our session came a worship leader who carried a bold, polished and professional sound that I could see was destined for stadiums. As he worshipped, I noticed his voice had a real impact on the nature of the meeting. His voice drew everyone within the facility into the worship space—a true gathering anointing. Yet when the next worship leader stepped up, everything shifted again. This worshippers smaller, more intimate voice didn't fill the room like her predecessor's, but it penetrated deep into the spiritual realm creating a holy and reverent atmosphere. While many left the room, I noticed it was the intercessors who remained, faces streaked with tears as they entered into deep intercession and communion with God. This worship carried the sound that unlocked intercession.

As the hours unfolded, we witnessed this pattern repeat: another worshipper, again with a stadium voice, would gather the masses seeing everyone gather in the room, while another's intercessory sound would activate the prayer warriors. Another worship leader operated like Elisha's minstrel, creating an atmosphere where prophetic words flowed freely. Each voice was distinct, each calling specific, each anointing essential for its purpose.

This revelation brings incredible freedom when we understand this principle: that attempting to emulate another's calling is futile and inevitably leads to frustration and spiritual striving. For what God wants to do in this season we need every worshipper to find their own unique voice and expression. Some are called to release their song over the family, some in their small prayer groups, some in their intercessory closet while others in stadiums and across the airwaves. No voice is more significant than others, and every voice is significant in their sphere of influence and place of mission. Not every worshipper is destined for a place on the platform. Some worshippers will have no audience at all except for an audience of one. What is your sound and where does it fit?

Territories of Influence

Every worshipper not only carries a unique expression but also holds divine authority over territories and areas that no one else can reach.

In order to impact the nation, worshippers must first start

PRACTICAL APPLICATION

Carrying the Presence Beyond the Church

Page 126

where they are, in the areas they can reach. This is why it's important for us to discern both the nature of our sound and the sphere of our influence. These territories of influence—whether homes, workplaces, or communities—become the battlegrounds and targets for releasing Heaven's frequencies, shifting the atmosphere and changing the hearts of people.

As a father in my household I carry the right to bring my sound to my home and family with authority like noone else can. As an employee I also have access to a range of people, situations and environments that one one else does. This is why it is important that we recognise our own spheres of influence. When we all operate effectively in our own areas we will have every base covered. You are the voice of breakthrough in your sphere of influence.

Releasing My Sound

My own journey as a school teacher has been an area in which I have been able to explore the release and impact of my own unique sound of worship. In my classroom, I've discovered that intentionally releasing worship through background instrumental playlists creates atmospheric shifts that significantly impacts the behaviour and mood of the students. During these lessons, students often benefit from this shift, with some even acknowledging that the sound carries Heavenly influence, asking "Sir, is this Christian music?". They can sense the presence of God on the music.

One particularly memorable instance occurred one day when a class was quite unsettled. One student cheekily said to me *"Sir, everyone's a bit noisy, you should go play the piano to settle everyone down"* Recognising a moment to be intentional about releasing the sound of worship, I went over and sat at the piano that is in the corner of the room. I intentionally positioned my heart to worship, and began to play. The students all know I can play the piano and have become accustomed to me taking brief moments to play here and there.

This particular moment as I began to play, I noticed an almost immediate shift in the atmosphere and also the students' behaviour within minutes. The previously unsettled and noisy environment began to settle and shortly after, most students were completely settled working on their project. I looked at the student who made the suggestion with a somewhat surprised smile. The student smiled back and gave an approving nod, acknowledging the shift in the atmosphere before putting their head back down to do their work.

This was a powerful example of releasing the sound of worship in a way that was covert. The gospel was not preached, and not a word was said, but the influence of Heaven through the sound of worship shaped the atmosphere and dynamic of the classroom. I have noticed over time, continuing with this strategy has opened up many conversations around faith and worship where I have been able to share openly.

Another area in which I have seen the power of worship have an impact was when I released a small instrumental worship album. This album gained influence in various areas including helping parents settle their children for bed and also helping others with the management of anxiety and stress. The most surprising was when the soundtrack found its way into a psychologist's waiting room, creating an atmosphere of peace in a place where people seek healing. The receptionist who would play it reported a noticeable shift in the atmosphere and also in the anxiety levels of her patients. The influence of worship in our homes, workplaces and beyond can be more powerful than we recognise.

Your Territory of Authority

These areas were my areas of influence… where are yours? Every believer holds unique territories of influence and authority where their worship can create breakthrough. Like David, who first worshipped in the fields before the palace, your sphere of influence is unique to you and somewhere only you can release the sound of worship. Thats why we need every worshipper to engage and infiltrate their surrounds.

It doesn't need to be with an instrument or with a song like my example. Perhaps it looks like a Spotify playlist playing in the background in your office or home. Perhaps it is by aligning your heart to worship and softly singing psalms, hymns and spiritual songs as you go about your day shifting the atmosphere around you. Perhaps playing Christian music in the room of your wayward teenager while they are at school or only listening to Christian radio in the car while the family is there. It all matters.

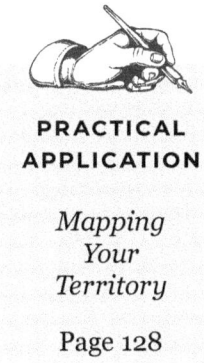

PRACTICAL APPLICATION

Mapping Your Territory

Page 128

The remarkable thing about Spirit-inspired worship music is that it carries the presence of God. When we are intentional about creating an atmosphere of worship, it will become a place of habitation for the Holy Spirit and a place of encounter for ourselves and for those around us.

So come on worshipper–release your song and change your world!

CHAPTER 10

The Call

As we come to the conclusion of this book, let's pause for a moment and dare to imagine. What would Australia look like if every worshipper was fully engaged and activated in their worship? Picture homes filled with the sound of praise, workplaces transformed by worship playing softly in the background, schools resonating with covert melodies, and churches unleashing their unique sound into their regions. Imagine every sphere of society being impacted by intentional, strategic worship. This is what we dare to dream about.

What if, like the armies of Jehoshaphat, we moved beyond merely singing songs to becoming a mighty force that determines battle outcomes and changing the destiny of the nation? What if, like David's tabernacle, we established places of continuous worship that transform entire cities? What if, like Paul and Silas, our praise became so powerful that it not only broke our own chains but also set others free and led to the salvation of entire families?

These aren't just inspiring stories from the past—they are blueprints for what God wants to do in our nation today. But here's the crucial truth: it requires every worshipper to take their place. Your voice, your sound and your expression is essential. There are atmospheres only you can shift, hearts only you can reach, and territories only you can impact through your unique sound of worship.

Consider your sphere of influence. What areas of your world are you called to shift? Is it your home, where daily worship could transform your family's atmosphere? Your workplace, where strategic worship music might soften hardened hearts? Your community, where your involvement in corporate worship could help build a canopy of praise over your region? These aren't just possibilities—they're divine assignments.

The days of lone rangers and one-man-bands are over. Every mighty move of God we see in Scripture came through unified worship. When Solomon's temple was dedicated, it was the unified sound that brought God's glory. When Jericho's walls fell, it was the unified shout that brought breakthrough. Every member must be vitally connected to the body in every way. To be powerful and effective it is important that every worshipper is:

- *Firmly planted in a local body, growing as part of the body.*
- *Submitted to spiritual leadership that can help nurture and direct their gift.*

- *In genuine relationship with fellow worshippers who can bring support, sharpening and encouragement*

A New Thing

The Lord is doing a new thing in this hour—it's a new season—do you perceive it? He's releasing fresh sounds that our ears have not heard before. These aren't just new melodies or contemporary expressions; they are Heaven-birthed frequencies that carry breakthrough power. Some will seem unusual, like the war cry that shifted an entire meeting's atmosphere. Others might appear insignificant, like a simple melody played over a classroom. But when released in obedience to Heaven's leading, they become mighty weapons in God's hands.

Australia, your time has come! The prophecies spoken over this Great Southland of the Holy Spirit are finding their fulfillment in this generation. But they require your participation. They need your sound. They await your release of Heaven's frequencies in your sphere of influence.

So arise, worshipper! Whether you're called to lead thousands or sing in your prayer closet, your sound matters. Whether your expression comes through voice, instrument, dance, or simply creating worship atmospheres, your part is essential. Don't hold back. Don't wait for someone else. Don't dismiss your role as

PRACTICAL APPLICATION

Your Response

Page 130

insignificant. The nation is waiting for your sound to be released.

Will you take your place? Will you join Heaven's orchestra? Will you be part of the mighty sound that shifts a nation?

The time is now! Rise up, worship warrior... your sound will shake the nation!

A Prophetic Declaration for the Nation

In submission to the authority of Jesus Christ, and in agreement with the prophetic destiny spoken over this Great Southland of the Holy Spirit, we declare:

- Let it be known in the heavens and declared in the earth that Australia's time has come! As it was declared in 1606, we affirm this land belongs to the Holy Spirit, and His presence shall flood every state, territory, and region from shore to shore.

- We declare the rising of God's worship army across this nation! From the Red Centre to the coastal cities, from remote communities to urban centers, a mighty sound of worship is being released. Every tribe, every tongue, every generation is taking their place in Heaven's orchestra.

- We declare that the prophetic sound of breakthrough is being released! Like Joshua's trumpets that brought down Jericho's walls, like David's harp that drove away tormenting spirits, like Paul and Silas's prison praise that broke every chain—so shall Australia's worship break ancient strongholds and usher in divine destiny.

- We declare that every home shall become a sanctuary of praise, every church a center of divine encounter, every workplace an outpost of Heaven's presence. No sphere shall remain untouched by the sound of authentic, Spirit-led worship.

- We declare the unlocking of new sounds from Heaven—prophetic songs, healing melodies, warfare anthems, and sounds of awakening. The uniqueness of every voice, the creativity of every instrument, the expression of every heart shall combine in a glorious symphony of praise that shifts the nation's atmosphere.

- We declare that unity is rising among God's people! Denominational walls are falling as worshippers unite under one banner. Like the musicians in Solomon's temple who sounded as one, Australia's worshippers are moving in supernatural harmony, creating a sound that brings Heaven's glory to earth.

- We declare that the wells of revival are being reopened! Ancient promises are being activated, generational prophecies are coming to fulfillment. The Spirit of God is hovering over this nation, waiting for the sound that will birth the greatest awakening in history.

- Let every demonic stronghold be torn down! Let every false altar be destroyed! Let every competing sound be silenced as the pure worship of Heaven rises from this Great Southland!

- We declare that Australia shall fulfill its prophetic destiny as a nation that releases the sound of revival to the ends of the earth. From this land shall flow rivers of living water, songs of deliverance, and sounds of transformation that impact nations.

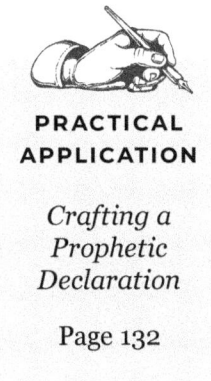

PRACTICAL APPLICATION

Crafting a Prophetic Declaration

Page 132

The time of preparation is over. The season of awakening is here. Australia, your sound of breakthrough has come!

"Arise, shine, for your light has come, and the glory of the LORD rises upon you!" –Isaiah 60:1 NKJV

So let it be written, so let it be done, in Jesus' mighty name!

Amen

SECTION 2

ACTIVATIONS

ACTIVATIONS

About These Activations

This section of the book is where the teaching in the previous chapters moves from inspiration to activation. The goal isn't just to learn about worship — it's to live it out. These activations are designed to help you take what you've read and put it into practical, transformative action — both in your personal worship and within your worship team or church community.

Whether you're working through these as an individual, a worship leader, or part of a team, this section will help you grow in confidence, boldness, and sensitivity to the Holy Spirit. Each activation invites you to engage with the content in a deeper way, applying it to your own life and the world around you.

ACTIVATION

Can My Worship Change a Nation?

2 Chronicles 7:14 NKJV — "If My people who are called by My name will humble themselves, and pray and seek My face, and turn from their wicked ways, then I will hear from heaven, and will forgive their sin and heal their land."

The book explores the idea that personal worship can shape nations. God often partners with individuals — like Moses, Esther, or David — to bring about national change. Your worship is not just personal; it carries authority to shift atmospheres and align regions with Heaven's will. Imagine the collective power of worshippers standing in agreement, releasing songs and prayers over their communities. God hears and responds.

- What areas of your community or nation need God's intervention?
- How can your personal worship become an intercession for those areas?
- How can we, as worshippers, intentionally pray for and worship over our city/nation?
- What stops us from believing our worship has this kind of authority?

PRACTICAL APPLICATION

Spend time in worship, declaring breakthrough over a specific area (e.g. family, church, or nation). Write down any impressions, Scriptures, or words you receive and be intentional about incorporating this is into your worship.

ACTIVATION

Hearing Heaven's Sound

Isaiah 42:10 NKJV — "Sing to the Lord a new song, and His praise from the ends of the earth."

The book highlights that breakthrough often requires a fresh sound — not just a repetition of the old. God calls His people to release "new songs" — sounds birthed from fresh revelation and intimacy with Him. These sounds carry a unique anointing, one that can shift the atmosphere and release Heaven's agenda.

- What "new song" might God want to birth in this season?
- Are you clinging to familiar sounds, or are you open to something fresh?
- How can we create space in worship for spontaneous, new sounds?
- What might hinder us from stepping into something new?

PRACTICAL APPLICATION

Spend some time intentionally asking God to reveal a new sound or melody. Perhaps he is breathing on an old song. Then be bold and sing or play whatever comes — no matter how unusual. What lyrics or songs does he bring to mind?

ACTIVATION

Singing Over Dry Bones

Ezekiel 37:4-5 NKJV — "Again He said to me, 'Prophesy to these bones, and say to them, 'O dry bones, hear the word of the Lord! Thus says the Lord God to these bones: 'Surely I will cause breath to enter into you, and you shall live.''"

Some situations in our lives and churches feel like dry bones — lifeless and hopeless. But God calls us to prophesy life into those places. Our worship can awaken dead dreams, broken relationships, or weary hearts. When we release faith-filled songs, we become a voice that calls dry bones to live.

- What area of your life feels like "dry bones"?
- How can you release life and hope over that situation through worship?
- How can we shift our worship to focus on releasing life over those areas?
- What Specific delcartions would you make to those "dry bones"?

PRACTICAL APPLICATION

Write a short, faith-filled chorus or declaration — something that speaks life to dead situations. Sing aand declare it as a prophetic act, declaring that dry bones will live again.

ACTIVATION

The Power of Declaration

Isaiah 55:11 NKJV — "So shall My word be that goes forth from My mouth; it shall not return to Me void, but it shall accomplish what I please, and it shall prosper in the thing for which I sent it."

God's Word never returns empty—it always produces results. When we intentionally declare His promises over our lives, we are releasing divine assignments into the earth. Our declarations are not wishful thinking; they are powerful weapons of agreement with Heaven. As worshippers, we must learn to release intentional, Spirit-led words that build, heal, and establish God's purposes.

- What are the areas of my life and beyond that I would like to see changed.
- What would change in my life if I believed every declaration had a divine assignment attached to it?
- What negative declarations or phrases do I need to repent of and replace with truth?
- How can you include bold and powerful declarations in your worship?

PRACTICAL APPLICATION

Write 3-5 declarations based on Scripture that speak directly to circumstances that need breakthrough. Declare them with faith regularly, evening truning them into song.

ACTIVATION

Worshippers as Priests

Scripture: 1 Peter 2:9 (NKJV) – "But you are a chosen generation, a royal priesthood, a holy nation, His own special people..."

In the Old Testament, priests stood in the gap between God and the people. In the New Covenant, worshippers still carry this priestly function — ministering to God and carrying His heart to the people. Worship isn't just personal; it's priestly. It has the power to intercede, to represent, and to reveal.

- What does it mean to take your place as a priest in worship?
- How does this understanding change the way you lead or participate in worship?
- In what ways are you interceding for your church or community through worship?
- What areas of your worship ministry need to be re-aligned with this priestly role?

PRACTICAL APPLICATION

List 3–5 people, families, or regions that God places on your heart. Commit to intercede for them during your personal worship time. As you sing or play, intentionally carry them before the Lord like a priest would carry the names of the tribes of Israel on their garments

ACTIVATION

Tuning In to His Voice

Scripture: John 10:27 NKJV — "My sheep hear My voice, and I know them, and they follow Me."

God is always speaking — the question is, are we listening? Sometimes His voice is loud and clear, and other times it's a gentle whisper. Either way God wants to speak and give direction for our lives.

- What has God been showing you or speaking to you about recently especially for this season?
- What is he showing for you personally and also for those around you (your teams, your homes etc)
- What scriptures reinforce what you believe God is saying.
- How do you think you can actively partner with Him in obedience with what he is saying?

PRACTICAL APPLICATION

Write down what you believe God is speaking to you about in this season. Ask him how to partner with it.

ACTIVATION

Sermons Into Songs

Pastors and leaders spend time seeking Heaven's heart, bringing forth sermons that are more than just messages — they're prophetic messages for the season. As worshippers, we have the powerful opportunity to turn those messages into songs that help carry the word of the Lord from head knowledge to heart revelation through song. When we echo the voice of our leaders in worship, we amplify Heaven's current agenda and give the congregation language to declare it.

- Do you recognise the prophetic weight in your leader's messages?
- How can you partner with those words both in personal and corporate worship?
- What are some of the recent themes or messages you could turn into song for your people?
- What would it look like to collaborate more closely with leadership to capture the sound of the house?

PRACTICAL APPLICATION

Take a recent sermon from your Pastor and identify key phrases or declarations that stand out. Brainstorm ways to turn that into a chorus or worship moment.

ACTIVATION

Partnering With Prophetic Words

1 Timothy 1:18 NKJV — "This charge I commit to you, son Timothy, according to the prophecies previously made concerning you, that by them you may wage the good warfare."

Prophetic words over nations and regions aren't just nice encouragements — they're blueprints for breakthrough. When we sing and declare those words in worship, we agree with Heaven and actively participate in bringing them to pass.

- What prophetic words have been spoken over you, your church, city, or nation?
- How can you partner with those words in worship?
- How can you help steward prophetic words through the songs you sing?
- What changes when we shift from singing about revival to declaring revival is here?

PRACTICAL APPLICATION

Find a trusted prophetic word with which to partner. Write a bold, faith-filled declaration or song that agrees with that word — then release it with faith and confidence, believing God will fulfill His promise and bring it to pass.

ACTIVATION

Writing The Songs For Tomorrow

Bill Johnson Quote: "Write the songs about it now, and we'll sing our way into it."

Bill Johnson's quote reminds us that worship isn't just a response to what God has done — it's a prophetic declaration of what He's about to do. Songs can pave the way into new seasons, stirring faith, hope, and boldness for what hasn't happened yet. Sometimes, we need to write the sound of the breakthrough before we ever see it. What if the songs you write today lead your church, city, or nation into revival tomorrow?

- What are you believing God for — in your life, your church, or your region?
- If you wrote a song about that breakthrough now, what would it say?
- What themes do we need to write and sing about for this season and the ones that are coming?
- How can we capture the sound of victory and breakthrough before we see it happen?

PRACTICAL APPLICATION

Brainstorm breakthrough themes of where you would like to see your church in 5 years time — revival, healing, unity, deliverance, etc. Write your ideas below. Now choose to be intentional about writing and singing the songs that will carry your church and your people forward into these areas.

ACTIVATION

The Sound of Unity

2 Chronicles 5:13-14 NKJV — "Indeed it came to pass, when the trumpeters and singers were as one... the house of the Lord was filled with a cloud."

The book explores unity — a key to hosting God's glory. When voices and sounds unify with Heaven's agenda, powerful things happen. We see this at Solomon's temple, where unified worship ushered in the tangible presence of God. Unity isn't uniformity; it's a harmony of diverse voices blending toward one purpose — to glorify Him.

- Is there any offense, pride, or division in your heart that needs addressing before you offer your gift at the alter? Take a moment to quietly pray, forgive and surrender them to God.
- Are there areas in your life where you could foster greater unity?
- What practical steps can you take to foster unity with those around you?
- What impact would complete unity have on worship in

PRACTICAL APPLICATION

Take a moment to pray for those around you. Write down one practical way you can support someone else's in releasing their portion. (e.g., encourage, mentor, or pray for them).

ACTIVATION

Carrying the Presence Beyond the Church

Scripture: 2 Samuel 6:11 NKJV — "The ark of the Lord remained in the house of Obed-Edom the Gittite three months. And the Lord blessed Obed-Edom and all his household."

God's presence isn't meant to stay within the church walls. When the ark of God rested in Obed-Edom's house, it brought blessing to his entire household. In the same way, our worship shouldn't stop at church — we are carriers of His presence everywhere we go.

- How aware of God's presence are you throughout the week, not just on Sundays?
- How can you create worship moments in your everyday environments — home, work, or community?
- How can you encourage others to stay mindful of His presence in daily life?
- What would our communities look like if we carried worship everywhere?

PRACTICAL APPLICATION

Consider how you will take worship with you beyond the church and beyond your own secret place. How will you do this? Will it be covert or will you worship openly? What do expect will happen?

ACTIVATION

Mapping Your Territory

Scripture: Joshua 1:3 NKJV — "Every place that the sole of your foot will tread upon I have given you, as I said to Moses."

God has given you spiritual territory — places, people, and spheres of influence where your worship carries authority. Recognizing your assigned territory helps you worship with greater boldness, knowing you're not just singing into the air — you're shifting the atmosphere over your domain.

- What areas of influence has God entrusted to you (home, workplace, church, city)?
- How can you impact those places in worship?
- What territories has our team or church been called to impact? (regionally, demographically, cultural etc)
- How can we pray and worship strategically over those areas?

PRACTICAL APPLICATION

Create a visual representation of your territories on influence. (ie. collage of images, printed map etc). Spend time worshiping and praying over each area, declaring God's presence and authority there. Write down what you believe God would want to do in those areas?

ACTIVATION

Your Response

Scripture: James 1:22 NKJV — "But be doers of the word, and not hearers only, deceiving yourselves."

Revelation without response leaves us unchanged. God doesn't just want to inform us — He wants to transform us. This book has stirred truths, challenged mindsets, and revealed new dimensions of worship and authority. Now, the question is: What will you do with it?

- What part of this book impacted you the most?
- What do you feel God is personally asking you to pursue or step into?
- What changes do you feel led to make in how you approach worship?

PRACTICAL APPLICATION

How will your worship change after you have ready this book? What do believe will be the impact of that change?

___
___
___
___
___
___
___
___
___
___
___
___
___
___
___
___
___
___

ACTIVATION

Crafting a Prophetic Declaration

Habakkuk 2:2NKJV — "2 Then the Lord answered me and said: "Write the vision and make it plain on tablets, That he may run who reads it."

Declarations are even more powerful when made together. Whether it's your family or worship team, standing united in a shared decree builds faith, unity, and expectation for what God is doing in and through you.

- What breakthrough or revival do you long to see for your family or team?
- How can you intentionally declare unity and purpose together?
- What prophetic promises or words has God spoken over you or your group?
- How can you turn those into a bold, collective declaration?

PRACTICAL APPLICATION

Write a decree that reflects vision God has for you. (e.g., "We declare our team carries the sound of Heaven — a sound that releases healing, freedom, and revival wherever we go!") Speak it together, and commit to declaring it regularly.

AUSTRALIAN **WORSHIP NETWORK**

"Equipping Worshippers, Empowering the Local Church"

Be **equipped** & **empowered** in your worship with AWN

Has this book stirred your heart to step into deeper, transformative worship? Are you ready to walk in greater authority and partner with God to see Him move in your home, region and the nation?

The Australian Worship Network and AWN School of Worship exists to equip and empower worshippers just like you. We provide training, practical and prophetic activation, and a community to help you step into new realms of worship with authority and power.

Can your worship change a nation? ***Yes it can!*** Join us today!

For more information visit
www.australianworshipnetwork.com.au